POEMS TO READ & DRAMATISE

Isi Agboaye, PhD

Step Out Creatives Publication

ISBN: 978-1-906963-18-7

For copies of this book, workshops and seminars,
Contact: isiagboaye@aol.com
Phone: +447817629683

Printed in Great Britain

TABLE OF CONTENTS

Introduction 1
Dedication 3
Dramatising the Poems 5
About the Poet 7
Who's your driver? 9
Coffee's pain 11
The Day I stopped combing my hair & wearing Jewellery 13
Children of Oppressors 16
The scourge of the Interpreters 18
Uninvited guests in my part of Africa 20
Growing inside the poor periphery 22
Punished for speaking Vernacular 23
The way we are 24
When we left the original Centre 26
Roaming in the periphery 28
Unfocused focus 30
Camera focussed 31
Point of no return 32

Cyber-Colonialism 34
Who's a Fool? 35
Power intoxicates.. 36
The African part of Heaven? 37
The one that lasts forever 38
Papa God, help us.. 39
Lies, more lies.. 41
If not God, who? 42
Being here.. 43
Sounds like old age 44
Baba prayer.. 45
Good children of bad gods.. 47
It's not an easy Road 49
What did you get for Christmas?.. 51
Oh Banana 52
Will they say, 'Happy New Year?' 53
The Parrot is caged at last.. 54
What we religious people say, and do.. 56
What really matters? 58
Teach me 59
Can I really marry you? 60
Death on dinner plates.. 61
The new African order.. 62
The Homeless one 63

Recreate the World 65
I hate writer's block 67
Like yesterday 69
Roll over, sleep 71
Wetin we de teach our children? 72
The sins of your factory 75
Governance is easy 76
Biafra 79
When people are bored in my part of Africa 80
Life 82
Nigerian revolution 83
Poor Child 86
Churches Everywhere 87
A version of the Creation Story 88
The Banana Tree speaks 90
I fear the 'silence' of God 91
Imagine Aliens on our Streets 93
Too late to be a Christian 95
Covid-19 - the real Terrorist 97
Is Brexit like the African 'Independence'? 99
Sabi Sabi 101
Emergency prayer meetings 103
Injuries in the periphery 105
Capacity for Sensitivity 106

Why is life like this? 107
Capacity for stress 109
Somebody said, 'Children in England are among the unhappiest in the world...' - BBC NEWS 110
We are all corrupt 112
Tiff Tiff - the thief 113
Capacity to forget 114
Capacity to know 115
Make you de tank God 116
Capacity to hate 117
Snap Narratives that people like in my part of Africa 118
The overzealous train inspector 120
The pain of self-Colonisation 122
What's the devil got to do with that? 124
Are we so different? 126
Too many Teachers 127
Decolonise & Develop 128
Picture my part of Africa 130
The Super pill 131
Matters Arising 134
Black Lives Matter 136
The Racist Test 137
Epiphany 138

INTRODUCTION

My intention here is to encourage the reader to look beyond reading the poems for pleasure; rather, to focus on how aspects of the poems may be applied in different ways. I also hope that the reader would be stimulated to activate the meanings in specific words or ideas that reflect social, economic, or political undertones that may be relevant for explaining the conditions of individuals and collectives embedded in the poems.

As the reader purposefully looks for elements of conflict in the poems, you are encouraged to dramatically push the limits of your imagination, touching on the socio-political and cultural issues reflected in the poems. It is anticipated that this would set the stage for a new level of experience, useful for creating or interrogating positive outcomes that makes drama assessable to more folks in the community.

As you read these poems, you would discover that whereas poems have hitherto been read for pleasure, the experience suggested in this text would instigate a wholistic performance approach that harnesses meanings which may be applied, interpreted, or conceptualised in various ways.

The whole experience is related to storytelling events in my part of Africa, suggesting that a tale narrated today may be different when narrated the following day because someone may have modified it to achieve a particular purpose. So, in my traditional part of Africa, if you want something to happen, you don't just sit and stare at words doing nothing; you simply activate the words that are presented to you. That's how great, meaningful, and colourful narratives that generate little and big changes are born before others came and forcefully changed things for us - making it seem as if we do not have any identity or belong anywhere.

DEDICATION

For Irekpitan my pretty grandma
Able to string words
Like a million Unuwazi beads
In few seconds

DRAMATISING THE POEMS

Since some of the poems are based on my area of research, postcolonial trauma in my part of Africa, I will suggest that you reflect on the various postcolonial elements and create narratives out of them touching on the implicit and explicit conflicts reflected in the poems.

I will advise that you freely pick aspects of the poems to dramatise or recite, with or without musical accompaniment. Also, there should be no cultural restrictions, knowing that the same issues explored in the poems may also be prevalent in other cultures and contexts.

You may use the poems as means of enacting a call and response performance. Thus, one person may read while another responds in songs or instrumentation; or two people may read a poem and interpret the embedded ideas orally with appropriate movements and gestures.

You may also dramatize aspects of the poems from a community drama perspective where the audience may be given the opportunity to deconstruct or apply aspects of the poems for the purpose of discovering more meanings that may be useful for explaining or understanding what is happening within a community.

ABOUT THE POET

Dr Isi Agboaye is a poet, playwright, and storyteller who studied at University of Jos, University of Ibadan, and the University of Wolverhampton where he obtained his PhD in Performing Arts. His research is focused on the exploration of postcolonial trauma in his part of Africa, Nigeria, and the diaspora for the purpose of gaining stimulus for playwriting and developing trauma-based plays. His playwriting experiments draw from African folktale contents and postcolonial concepts as underpinning for explaining and understanding the plight of Africans in the continent and the diaspora. He hopes to find a voice for writing and producing plays that highlight decolonization and development. He has served as visiting lecturer in Creative Writing and Drama at University of Wolverhampton and Bishop Grosseteste University, Lincoln.

Who's your driver?

Wait
Think twice before you vote
With your head
Not your fingers
Soiled again and again
Bribed and bought
Corrupted
By politicians
Claiming they know
Driving the bus
To the rocks
Crashing whole destinies
Again, and again

Wait; listen to new instructions

You've got a head
Your fingers, not doomed
Not soiled
Not willing
To be soiled
Bribed, bought
Corrupted
By politicians
Claiming they know

Driving the bus
To the rocks
Crashing whole destinies
Again, and again

Coffee's pain

Ruba:
Our friends the farmers
Returned
Crumpled
Famished
Impoverished

Koko:
Our friends
The farmers
Returned
Watching
Hoping
Praying

Ruba:
Praying
Concerning
The price
But the meeting
Adjourned
The BBC woman
Spoke staccato
Gliding on
Her stiletto

Koko:
Concerning
Our status,
We're still
Depressed
Totally oppressed
Hardly prospered
Not showcased
Not celebrated

Ruba:
The farmers returned
Deflated
Demoralised
The world
Raised millions
Of coffee cups
Echoing,
'More Coffee please'

The Day I stopped combing my hair & wearing Jewellery

I had a vision
Of my grandfather
Popular slave driver
In those days
Rich; filthy ignorant
Very arrogant
Saying
See my comb
See my smoking pipes
See my mirrors
See my coloured stones
See my wives
Dancing around me
In my big house, flashy

I stand wondering
How him bargained
With the oyibo man
All the way from England
Slaves exchanged
Fortune smiling
For him only
Souls languishing
In squalor all around him

Grieving
I had another vision
Of my big uncle
Popular like my grandfather
In these days
Rich; filthy ignorant
Also arrogant
Saying
See my foreign cigars
See my cars
See my watches
See my precious stones
See my girlfriends
Dancing around me
In my big house, flashy

I stand wondering
How him bargained
With the oyibo man
All over the world
Citizens oppressed
Fortune smiling
For him only
Souls languishing
In squalor all around him
Grieving

So, I stopped combing my hair
I stopped wearing Jewellery
I started speaking about change
I started hating the evil wind
Blowing around them
Blustering their nakedness

Children of Oppressors

They invade the circle
Like their parents did
Taking over
Dancing more vigorously
Than their parents
Claiming every inch
Claiming every mile
Claiming every space

We stand
Bewildered in shock
Watching; complaining
Like fools
Drained
Drained of all meaning
Like our parents,
Drained
Drained of all knowledge
As we stand
Watching

They invade the circle
Like their parents
Taking over
Dancing more vigorously

Than their parents
Claiming every inch
Claiming every mile
Claiming every space

The scourge of the Interpreters

It's not the whips of the new masters
That mattered most
It was the words
Words of their interpreters
Our own flesh
Our own blood
Puking vile actions
Laced with bile
And hate
Crashing on us
Like a thousand thunders
To please their masters
To hurt us deeply

No wonder
The masters loved them dearly
Blessing them with
Strange names,
So irritating
Truly irritating
Then they pestered us
With new taxes,
More bills

Then they died,
Their children took over
As senior civil servants
Spitting fire,
Withholding our Salaries
For months
For many months
Why?

Uninvited guests in my part of Africa

Our people
Have arrived
Who's
Looking at faces?
Some sing
Some dance
Some bearing goodies
Dancing and singing off-key

The hosts
Can't compete
They've
Taken the seats
Flowing
With
The drinks
Thoroughly linked
To the Kitchen

Ever patient
Hosts
Replenishing
Fresh foods
Seasoned

Garnished
For
Everyone.

I'm picturing
The uninvited,
Smiling
More than
The invited
That's
How we are
They will dine
Celebrate
Break plates
Say long prayers
Then depart
Then return
For the next celebration

Growing inside the poor periphery

Inside the periphery
You may think
Nothing happened
But everything happened

Our roofs leaked terribly
Our floors gushed tears
Our pockets leaked sorely

When thoroughly hungry
We lapped water
From rain drops
Or frustrated streams
With germs
But they are not
Bread and fish

At night,
Hunger echoed widely
Who could sleep like that?
We were scared stiff
Scared of returning
Returning to another day
Yet, we did

Punished for speaking Vernacular

How the class monitor snitched on us for speaking vernacular
How our parents screamed at us
For speaking English at home
How the community must decide
What I should do
Speak English
Or speak vernacular

How my lunch money was taken
By the class monitor
How I missed part of my dinner
For speaking English at home
How the government must decide
What I should
Or should not speak

So,
You must call my class monitor
You must call my parents
You must call the government
To explain
Why I must speak English
Why I must speak vernacular
So, how do I feel now?

The way we are

The way we are
Today,
Tomorrow
Forever?

We're waiting
By the deaf gate
Inspired and waiting
By deaf walls, waiting

The community calls
Though fractured
Goodness echoes
Junctions abandoned
Taken over by others

The nation
Stands silent
Suspended
Trying to understand
Yet, trapped by walls

The leaders
All speak the same
The same

Wish they can see
The beauty
Of the community
The open un-trapped
Wilderness, calling

None understands
Not the children
Not the elders
Not the men, or women
None

When we left the original Centre

Then they said
If you want to gain knowledge
Come to our school
It must be our school
Or nothing else
Come to our school
You'll know everything

Then they said
If you want to be entertained
Come to our theatre
It must be our theatre
Or nothing else
Come to our theatre
We know exactly what you like

Meanwhile,
The village square lay abandoned
No echoes of voices
Calling children to play
No forming of circles
Or creation of stories

We're all trapped
Behind walls floating

With thoughts we don't understand
With thoughts we don't need
With thoughts we can't apply
Then, taught to hate each other
Daily
Why?

Roaming in the periphery

Since things fell apart
We have been floundering
Floundering in the periphery
Watching, as
Foreign oppressors
And their home agents
Stay in the core
Then and now
Perhaps, forever

Since things fell apart
We suffer loss
Stuck in the periphery
Stripped of hope
Saddled with loans
Circling, confused, drunk
With Independence beer
Mixed with Corruption
Perhaps, forever

Since things fell apart
We have been counting
Corpses in the Sahara Desert
Our children, wondering
Singing sad songs

Cursing Independence
Yet, we dance
Disconnected
We chant
So unconnected
In this condition
Who's talking of stability
Who's talking, talking
Of accountability?

Unfocused focus

You chop
You look oyibo
You belch
You look oyibo
You piss
You look oyibo
You shit
You look oyibo
You read book
You look oyibo
You smile
You look oyibo
You cry
You look oyibo
You fall for gutter
You look oyibo
You come out
You look oyibo
Oyibo see you?
No

Camera focussed

If you,
Look long enough
Continuously
Firmly
Not
Casually
Not
Slightly
Not
One quick glance
Or faint reaction
Unfocussed
But a piercing look
Fixed
Directed
Firmly fixated
Stuck solid
You'll snap gold
You'll see God
You will
You certainly will

Point of no return

When the in-laws visited
To greet the bride's family
And possibly to take her home
They were mesmerised, as
Proper Nigerian roasted yams
Waited; announced
Palm oil and pepper
Greeting bitter-leaf
No one complained
Unfinished business
Curtailed sharply, as
A thunderous applause
Greeting the entrance
Of pounded yam
Sensibly positioned
Pretty girls serving
Ohiele soup, bitter-leaf soup
Egusi-soup, fish, meat,
Assorted combinations
No one complained
They feasted, feasted
Like forever
Then the palmwine arrived
Fresh palmwine;
Undiluted; it flowed

Like forever and ever
Then the main item;
The bride-price
The groom was intimidated
Checking his pocket
Again, and again
Wondering if he should run and hide
Then the old father whispered,
The young men understood
Pointing to his car
Bags were hurled in
Cowries
Plenty Cowries
More Cowries
Silence
The elders have spoken
The mothers began to sing
The old father began to dance
Others joined in
At this stage, they had reached
The point
Of no return

Cyber-Colonialism

This is the place
Where we're
Not just decolonised
But properly colonised
Evil minds
Taking
All we've got

This is the place
Where ignorance sticks
Where we evolve
Into something else
All morality
Take flight
We, acting civilised

This is the place
Some play God
Some change skins
Trade words, insult elders
Share trash, without cash

This is the place
We spread secrets
We lost self; self lost us
We lost God; God lost us
In the crowd

Who's a Fool?

You called him a fool
He did not attend your local school
He did not obtain your posh degrees
Yet, he does not know
That he does not know
Neither interested in knowing

One day, he gets nominated
He sits on our wealth
We are angry
He's got police escort
He's got the beautiful girls
He's got the streets
Named after him
What can we do?

Power intoxicates

Watch others, displaying power
In tiny offices, on roadsides
Even the peanut vendors
Intoxicated with power
Like drunkards spirited

Watch others, like the bus conductor
The ticket collector, the gateman
All drunk, issuing orders
After a sip of power
In a trip so elongated

A little opportunity, over manifested
Reminds me of politicians
Crawling and begging
All for your votes
Then they win,
Then bite you
Then spit you out

The African part of Heaven?

You just arrived
No God, no angels
No golden roads
Same police
Bribery fortified
There's no throne
Of mercy
No outpouring
Of grace
No fragment
Of hallelujah
No unity, more strife
Nothing works
Electricity blinks
All unpaid workers
On permanent recess
The water system
So contaminated
Generators booming
Ear plugs stinking
Of overuse
No mansions, no industries
You kneel, praying
Knowing fully
You are still colonised

The one that lasts forever

Poor you, looking
At Facebook, Twitter
Snapchat; hmmm
Look beyond
The glitter
They blister tomorrow
The red or pink lips
They mess your vision
The accursed wink
They blind your judgement
The feigned walk
They twist your ideas
The sweet sweet words
They are loaded with lies
Look for reality
Look for
Akara, Agidi and Akpu
Home-bred stuff
No mixture
Pure Agbo-gidi
No silky talk
That's where truth lies
That one is made to last

Papa God, help us

How de thing happen?
Abi you first create us?
Tabi na oyibo you create first?
Then you come add dem?
Abi na we you add?
Why papa, why?

Who first come here?
Na we
Or na oyibo man?
Why him de drive us
Everywhere
Why papa, why?

We de our country
E bring wahala
We go him country
E bring wahala
Plenty wahala
Why papa, why?

Oyibo man sabi God?
Oyibo man sabi our suffer?
We de follow like mumu
Wear him dress

De smell like rubber
Why papa, why?

Papa God, I beg
You fit create another world
Just for us
Just for us only?
We go hold praise party
Praise you forever

Lies, more lies

One lie
Another lie
More lies
Forever lies
Piled up lies
Linking with lies
Overtaking lies
Projecting lies
Forever lies
Well baked slices of lies
Buttered lies
Eaten between lies
Digested as lies
Forever, lies
One lie
Another lie
More lies
Forever lies

If not God, who?

How he locks you in
So evil may pass
How one door closes
So you may learn
How he lets you cry
So you may laugh
How he blocks old paths
So new paths may cross
How he changes plans
So you can soar
How he let's you crawl
So you may run
Hmmm,
How he's always God
So I will be me
If not God,
Then, who?

Being here

I am here, not there
Because I am here
Otherwise,
I would be there
Sometimes,
I don't know
Why I am here
But I am here
Sometimes,
I wonder
Why I am here
With you
And you, and you
Sometimes,
I am listening
Sometimes,
I am learning
Learning
To be here, not there
Learning to know
Why I am here

Sounds like old age

Yesterday it was the neck
Today, what the heck?
Tomorrow, back pain
This is not like me
The ear drum rings
Sometimes a shrill
Sometimes it's a bang
Then the waist
Reports for duty
Stubbornly
Refusing to mop the floor
Or touch the toe
What?
Don't talk about press ups
As I am watching the acts,
The hearing aid arrives
I can't even read
The instructions
The ear drum rings
It's not the devil
It's me, talking to me

Baba prayer

Our Baba
Na you de heaven
I throway salute
Na you de in charge
Nobi some people
Whe think say dem be God
I no ask for daily bread
I only ask say
No let me eat plastic rice
No let me eat human suya
No let me jam stone
No let me jam police
Forgive all the bad things
I de do everyday
I don try try,
I no fit do good
Na only you good
Not even my village fada
Helep me forgive others
Dem own too much
Dem wahala carry load
You sabi say
I no like wahala
Help me
Make I no enter temptation

Make I no follow evil
Weda by lookery
Weda by touchery
Weda by talkery
Na you get everything
Na you get power
Na you fit born person
Na you fit kill person
I throway salute again
I beg catch am, bless me, amen

Good children of bad gods

You are dancing again
We are clapping for you
You are spinning our minds
Hush
You are barking again
You are spraying money again
We are being crushed again
Hush
You are saying it all
We can't speak our minds
You are the god of all
Hush
You are cursing our names
We are praising your name
You are saying amen
Hush
You are drinking Champagne
We are getting unpaid
You are ordering some more
Hush
We are travelling on roads
You are flying above
We are voting for you
Hush
You are eating salad

You are eating pepper soup
We are drinking garri
Hush
We are praying for you
We are voting for you
You are sitting on us
Hush
You are saying we are fools
You are thinking we are done
We are seeing your tricks
Hush
We are waiting for you
We are gathering our stones
You will be hearing from us
Hush

It's not an easy Road

We are travelling to paradise and singing cocky songs like it's a smooth ride on a golden road with no potholes.

We are wearing torn jeans, saggy pants and jolted miniskirts, jumping around the pews with the better parts of us dangling, accompanied by the latest steps construed from the pits of who knows where?

Pausing for ice water, sugar candies and high-fives we turn around to see who was watching and if we had really impressed the stadium.

The hymns are hardly inspiring, so we have invented high class rocks to ferry us to the gates of paradise as we shout hallelujah in phonetic dimensions and proportions.

Who touched me? I asked and asked again because we want to be touched by those who matter and not some riff-raff who must not share our pew structures.

We must be boasting about our pastors and the wonders they can perform forgetting that someone on a non-psychedelic cross did it all. On the other hand, the leaders must be competing and showing off their latest wonders forgetting that those who compare themselves to themselves are not, what?

It's the end of the service and non-worshippers of other faiths have to teach us how to love the brethren; but we must tell lies winding up our car windows because we don't want to travel for an extra mile. Why?

It's not an easy road; someone bore the scourge; ask the disciples and Apostles of old. Someone died to give you that name and status. So, why do you think you can just glide into his paradise singing easy songs, eating ice cream with a variety of sex toys in your pocket?

He was trashed, bruised, battered, disgraced, disrespected; what else? I ask for mercy, not judgement, but hoping we would appreciate that it's not an easy road that we are travelling to paradise, made possible through the pain of one great man; so unassuming. Hopefully, there's still time to ask for mercy.

What did you get for Christmas?

(Inspired by one NHS advert on a bus)

Did you get
An unplanned pregnancy
Or HIV
Or were you
So, so excited
That you got
Dreadful Chlamydia
With its friend
Gonorrhoea?
Or did you get
So drunk
That you bagged
Herpes and
Syphilis?

He got Gold, Frankincense
And Myrrh; and miserable
Stable; because
There was no room
In the best Hotel
Where you lodged

Oh Banana

On sighting you
This morning
I am inspired.
Thinking
Of your simplicity
Of your felicity
Of your flexibility
Makes me wonder
As you meander
From forest farms
Shaking hands
With monkeys
With peasants
Then you travelled
To the table
Of the rich, of the poor
Of presidents, of Queens
Giving no room
To discrimination
Like Others
I greet you
Oh Banana
The bounteous
Green or yellow
Spectacle

Will they say, 'Happy New Year?'

From morning to evening
In one miserable farm
Somewhere
In Africa

Picking tea
Picking cashew
Plucking Cocoa
For your pleasure

From morning to evening
In one miserable farm
Somewhere
Working hard
For your pleasure

For such kids
School closed
Hope constricted
Poverty opened the door
Maybe you don't know
Or pretend not to know;
Child abuse
On your conscience

The Parrot is caged at last

That's the parrot
Trapped
Trapped at last
Caged
Caged and crushed.

That's the parrot
That was free, happy
Blooming blessed
Cruising freely
From height to height
Reaching miles
In a minute

That's the parrot
Now drenched soggy
By horrid words and deeds
Of mankind
Tortured trite
By their ferocious pride
As they toss
The unwilling bird
From here to there
Poked sore
In their weird doctrines.
In unconscious submission

All songs gone
Grieving to the core
Yet, hoping to be freed
By Oise's word
God's magic command
Planted in the depth
Of her weary soul.

What we religious people say, and do...

Like
Thinking we know God
When we don't know
Our neighbour
Or care how they feel
I wonder
Like
Asking the devil
To go to a wrong address
When that address
Is clearly
Our neighbour's house
I wonder
Like
Telling the devil
To get behind us
When someone
Was standing behind
I wonder
Like
Pointing to others
When other fingers
Point at us
So clearly

I wonder
Like
Looking up to heaven
When heaven
Surrounds us,
Deeply inside us
I wonder

What really matters?

Know yourself
Better than
You know the road
Know your strength
Better than
You know the task
Know others
Better than
You know the map
Not that
You don't need
The road
Your task
The map
But friend,
You would do well
If you know
Others better

Teach me

If you teach me
I will know it
If you show me
I will fix things

But you sit there
Asking questions
Waiting
Wishing
That I stumble
That I fumble
That you may laugh

But I am still humble
If you teach me
I will know it
If you show me
I will can fix things

Can I really marry you?

Can I cook for your
Elephant appetite?
And add spices
That warm
Your nostrils?
Can I accept
Your criticism
And forgive you
Again and again?
Am I patient
Kind
And ready?
Can I play
With you
Like a friend
Plaiting your hair
And watching
You grow old?

I don't know
I don't really know
I don't have the certificate
No experience
So, I will stay in my house
As you stay in your house

Death on dinner plates

They just served you
Plastic rice
Sourced from
Death's backyard
They just served you
Champaign
Brewed
From their urine
Sparkling
As for the
Corned beef
Questions
Questions
As the Undertakers
Are loaded with cash
Racing
To the bank
Returning
To kill more

The new African order

When you're all
Tired, of being
Bossed, tossed
By the superpowers
Posing as gods
You will consider
People-ocracy

You will welcome
House of the women
House of the men
House of the youths
No salaries
No foolish bills
No long cars
No long speeches

Wake up
Smell your poverty
Smell your foolishness
Smell your backwardness
Smell their wickedness
Play real politics
Serve the people

The Homeless one

Yesterday
Like today
You sat
Gazing
Into no future
You were warm
So cosy, at birth
From warm
Blankets
To freezing
Blankets
You are
Quivering
Hugging
The November
The December
Cold
Battered
By the
January
February
Cold quivering
I saw
The Teacher
The Banker
In your eyes

You were denied
Dismissed
Distracted
I don't know
Then I wanted to help
You sneered
I wondered
Maybe
I should have asked-
Where is home?

Recreate the World

It seems
Like
There's
One God
For the east
One God
For the west
It seems
Like
There's
One God
For the rich
One God
For the poor
It seems
Like
There's
One God
For the Oyibo
One God
For the Dudu
Dear God,
You don't
Need my help?
I could volunteer

In the
Casting
Carving
Chip
Chip
Here, there
Hopefully
All will be fixed
Fixed into
A brand-new world

I hate writer's block

Even
Juggernauts
Or
Whatever
With powers
Massed
Can't
Tune this thing
Or change things
Blocked
Blocked
Or bang
The keys
Of that
Computer, or
Typewriter
Now
Blocked
Blocked
Not a word
Not an idea
All ideas
All business
All drama
Blocked

Blocked
They've
Travelled
To yonder
Minds
You are
Waiting
Waiting
So,
Who will you call?
Who?
Who?
Who?

Like yesterday

Your admonitions
Were coded in words
As we walked
From big or small markets
Pathways, marked
By experiences

Sometimes, I would sit, listening
But watching the early stars
You thought I had drifted off
Wondering amiss
Then, dad would appear
Touching on the names
Of stars in Esan
And their formations

I thought stars
Were holding their meetings
In the sky everyday
He told his tales quickly
Then disappeared

So, you took over
Working through
Narratives

Upon narratives
Now echoing in my mind
All coded in tones
Mindfully coloured
For future performances
The tales had an end
As we continue talking
In our dreams, wondering
Still learning, still knowing
The difference between
This or that

Or why this plant or root
Must do this or that
With this or that bark
Of this or that tree
Did not do what
Or, why others
Didn't do what
They're supposed
To do, because of
This or that.

Roll over, sleep

Then,
There was Saul
Carousing with evil
Handing the sword
To one Hitler
And Mussolini
And the slave raiders
Where are they now?
When God created peace
He thought about you
When God created sleep
He thought about you
Why are you now
Afraid of threats, and
Pronouncements
As the Storm trumpets fear
Calling for battle
Thundering
Flashing lightening
Worry wrapping
The hearts of many
Fear not
Roll over,
Sleep soundly
It will not last

Wetin we de teach our children?

Aba:
Others de do SCIENCE
De laugh, de laugh
Dem de do EXPERIMENTS
De laugh, de laugh
Dem de change the World
De laugh, de laugh

Oko:
You de teach your children
To sidon de cry
De cry, de cry
You de teach your children
To sidon de cry
Dem still de cry

Aba:
Others de go SPACE
De laugh, de laugh
Dem de do EXPERIMENTS
De laugh, de laugh
Dem de on top the World
De laugh, de laugh

Oko:
You de teach your children
To sidon de cry
De cry, de cry
You de teach your children
To sidon de cry
Dem still de cry

Aba:
Others de do ELECTRIC CAR
De laugh, de laugh
Dem de do EXPERIMENTS
De laugh, de laugh
Dem de progress big big
De laugh, de laugh

Oko:
You de teach your children
To sidon de cry
De cry, de cry
You de teach your children
To sidon de cry
Dem still de cry

Aba:
Others get ARTIFICIAL INTELLIGENCE
De laugh, de laugh
Dem de do EXPERIMENTS

De laugh, de laugh
Dem de see tomorrow
De laugh, de laugh

Oko:
You de teach your children
To sidon de cry
De cry, de cry
You de teach your children
To sidon de cry
Dem still de cry

The sins of your factory

Your factory
Is belching
Sinful smoke
Strangling
Our lungs

They are puking bile
Into our once
Pure rivers

Again, again
You said nothing

But,
When
You found words
You echoed,
That's progress
That's development

Governance is easy

Don't let them fool you
Governance
Is easy
So easy

You don't need
Padded
Constitutions
Or padded
Instructions
Dressed as budgets

You don't need
Sleeping-legislators
Or looters
Or spoilers
And appendages
And limousines
In Africa

You don't need
Balancing
Of budgets
Balancing of Grammar

We produce
We export
We bank the money
We bank the money

Who's hungry?
None.
Who's homeless?
None
Who's kidnapping?
None

We produce
We employ
We tax
We produce
We employ
We tax

We make more money
All eyes
Watching the money

We make more money
All eyes
Watching the money

That's Government of the people
That's Government by the people
That's Government for the people

Biafra

If you do not destroy yourselves
With stupid arguments
And bickering blocks
You will soon see
That your enemy is not Goliath
But the tiny foxes
Of petty pebbles
Crippling the camp
You will soon see
That victory is possible
As your sun will rise
Showing the path of freedom
To the rest of Africa

When people are bored in my part of Africa

They
Argue around newspaper stands
Vote with their toes
Then steal the ballot box
Not Installing the winner
They
Discuss foreign politics
Support Donald Trump
Wish they're Americans
Speaking through their nostrils
They
Marry more wives
Call the old one a devil
Send her away to suffer
With six or ten kids
They
Cry about foreign exchange
Crave imported foods
Curse the devil and government
For all their woes
They
Start a church
Start other branches
But can't start a farm

Complaining of hunger
They
Moan all day, pray all day
Hate the government
Yet afraid to take action
Acting like they know it all
They
Praise and reward the criminals
Execute poor hungry thieves
Set fire on them with tyres
Proclaiming jungle justice
They
Get appointed, celebrate forever
Refuse to pay salaries
Dance and spray cash
Acting like they don't care

Life

This labyrinth
Snaking
In
Sneaking
Out
You cost a lot
You caused a lot
You tug
You torture
You terminate
Are you laughing?
And watching?
Many, moaning
Misery stricken
Begging
For simple bread
For simple water
What's you secret?
Known by these few,
Now stripped
Of all knowing
Struck;
I am perplexed.

Nigerian revolution

E no possible jo
You shoot gun, dem go run go hide
Some de chop money for corner
Dem go collect am go hide de enjoy am
Who no get sense?

The awareness no de there
If na real revolution
E go happen gbam
E go be like say people don tire
Dem don tire reach sky
No turning back
Hmmmm

As e be now
South east de talk one thing
East de talk dem own
North get dem own story
Middle belt de burn fire
West de Sidon de look
Who go take action?

As e be now
E be like say
Our people still like to suffer.

If you shout for dem head,
Dem go hold prayer for 30 days
Dem go de bind Satan
Oppression de bulala dem
Satan just de laugh
Him no get hand for the matter
Him no steal money
Him no de government
Him no be minister
You de bind the wrong guy jo.

As e be now
If you lie to them,
Dem go grumble small,
Pray again and sing choruses
Dem go de manage.
Dat kind person go do revolution?
Naaaaaa.
So who wan go face bullet?

As e be now
Oppression full ground,
We sabi; but our people
Like to suffer
Na dem collect salt
Na dem collect stockfish
Na dem collect money to vote
How dem go revolt?
Naaaaa.

As e be now
Dem don buy dem power
Dem don sell dem vote
We been warn dem
Dem still de hungry
Dem must suffer in silence.
Dem go say, make we manage;
One day, e go better.
As for say make dem revolt,
Naaaa, e no go happen
E no go happen.
The time never reach

Poor Child

You spoilt that child solely
Moulding a belligerent bully
You quip; my child is a saint'
They're using the wrong paint
Not a computer armed constrictor?
Not a merciless mocker?
Here, feel the shocks
That's him in everlasting stocks

Churches Everywhere

Churches on every street
Every member,
A potential pastor
Anger is free
You annoy me, I start my own
Churches in every compound
Every pastor,
A president-founder
Pride is free
If you correct me, I start my own
Churches everywhere
Love is scarce
Christians fighting Christians
Others laughing or confused
Churches everywhere
Change is rare
Purity travelled
Holiness in trickles
Churches everywhere
We can sing choruses
We can steal offering buckets
We're slippery like fish
The Gospel
Still the Gospel
The truth, still the truth
We're still not saved

A version of the Creation Story

Check the instruction manual
We are supposed to punch holes
Specific holes
I'll speak the instructions
Be attentive
Drill

Where?
Drill the front of the head
Move slightly down
Drill; it's important
One outlet
For speaking
For drinking
For chewing

What else?
Drill the front of the head
Move slightly above
Drill; it's important
Two outlets
For breathing
For smelling

What else?
Move further down
Further down
Water pipe; done
Procreation pipe, done
Drill behind
Careful
Pipe for evicting stuff
Even windy stuff

Looks so perfect
Nothing else to do
Nothing to add
It's been hectic

Any more holes?
None; all done
No; we forgot the ears
Drill; two holes
Drill carefully
One on each side
Done

Now it will hear everything
We forgot the eyes
Drill; carefully
Drill the eyes too
Now it will see everything
Including the apple

The Banana Tree speaks

I will wave at you as you pass by my house.
You can cut a branch and call it your umbrella as it rains.
You can cut another branch and freely wrap your ingredients in the market.
You may cut another branch and wrap your food, touching on a new flavour that I provide freely.
You can cut another branch as additional ingredient to your medication to heal your broken bones.
What else do you want?
You may come next year and pluck the bunch of banana - all free.
Don't forget to cut my stem, so I can keep growing, growing, so you can use me as much as you like.

I fear the 'silence' of God

We are waiting
In different postures
Soiled; self-soiled
Wondering, all maligned
Totally self-opinionated
I'm thinking
Is he going to rain rocks
Or acid fire; as folks
Blatantly conspire
Defiling all goodness?

Hear their megaphones echoing
Echoing in whose sanctuary?
Your house really?

They are interpreting your will
Your sanctified meanings
Dramatising divinity
Playing God; contradicting
Their own interpretations
Claiming your heritage
In books upon books
In words upon words
Credited and dominated
By others; still

You're silent, watching
Silent
I fear your silence.

Imagine Aliens on our Streets

In tens
In twenties
Then in hundreds
They stormed
Every street and city

Tired of pointing
Weary torches
Hovering and wondering
They're here at last

We're demobilised
Frozen stiff
Even the best of us

All military halted
Not a dog barking
All governments halted
Not one bullet fired

Aliens roaming freely
Laughing freely
What decadence
They thought
Reading our minds

Scorning our Science
Like stuff they saw
Millions of years ago

We finally wake up from
Their induced slumber
We continued civilisation
Same civilisation

Their laughter echoed
Bursting eardrums
As they drifted away
Still laughing

Where are your
Listening devices?
Crap, stale
useless

Too late to be a Christian

Harbour animosity
Find a Bible verse
To suppress it
Pray about it
Settled

Compare pulpits
Pile all the wealth
Refuse to share
Ignore the poor
Settled

Harbour wickedness
Find a Bible verse
To legitimise it
Pray about it
Settled

Speak diverse tongues
Victimise unbelievers
Judge the brethren
Reinvent the Bible
Settled

Mock the preacher
Pick bones in all sermons
Refuse to understand
Scorn and scorn
Settled

Get to heaven's gate
Books are opened
The end at last
Too late to repent
Settled

Covid-19 - the real Terrorist

You're so viciously invisible
Operating callously
Taking over cities
Silence visiting streets
Creating terrible lockdowns
Who declared a war?

You walk through hospitals
Without guns
Without bombs
Wrenching lives
Boldly, aggressively
Are we amused?

You're terrorising companies
You're terrorising families
You're terrorising nations
Economic meltdown staring
As planes fly empty
Why?

We can't sneeze freely
Hand sanitisers; all exhausted
Toilet paper, all exhausted
We're panic shopping

Behold, the end of the world
So soon?

We are all mesmerised
Stupefied by your antics
Some say this
Some say that
None can read you
None

We can't trap you either
Not even our best scientists
Not even the politicians
Can decode your motives
Or guess your ransom; none.
Why?

Are you laughing cynically
Behind that horrible mask
Teasing and taunting us?
We are still washing our hands
Waiting to quarantine you

Is Brexit like the African 'Independence'?

What's this Brexit wahala?
Who's afraid of DEAL
Or no DEAL?
Who's afraid of soft
Or HARD Brexit?
Please explain it to me.

Is it like
Our HARD 'Independence'
With lingering pains
Loaded with DEALS
And confused DEALS?
Please explain it to me.

What's the BACKstop?
Is it like sneaking
Into Europe by land?
Or dem dumping toxic goods
In our markets?
Please explain it to me.

What is soft Brexit?
Is it like foreign investors
Milking and crushing

Grabbing our resources
For a penny?
Please explain it to me.

Sabi Sabi

Sabi Sabi
Na so so talk talk
You talk for here
You talk for there
You talk everywhere
You talk wetin dem ask you
You talk wetin dem no ask you
You talk talk
You carry yourself enter wahala

Sabi Sabi
Your mouth de leak
Your tank don burst
Leak for here
Leak for there
You talk wetin dem ask you
You talk wetin dem no ask you
You talk talk
You carry yourself enter wahala

Sabi Sabi
You be like radio the wire don cut
You talk de talk
You forget yourself
Even self, market don finish

You talk wetin dem ask you
You talk wetin dem no ask you
You talk talk
You carry yourself enter wahala
Sabi Sabi
You sidon de talk
Talk and talk
Everybody don reach home
You bend your mouth
You talk wetin dem ask you
You talk wetin dem no ask you
You talk talk
You carry yourself enter wahala

Emergency prayer meetings

You're surrounded
Your enemy, like a familiar
Spirit reads you
Like a book, cleverly
Setting you up
One against another

You hate your generals
You're so church-fussy
You analyse falsely
All for un-buttered bread
All for frustrated stockfish
Given by Satan's agents

You vote wrongly
You pick wrongly
Helping to craft
Outcomes, so bleak
You keep calling on God, God
Like them prophets of Baal

Would you face reality?
Would you work functionally?
No; you're busy in disunity
Would you fix your mess?

No; you are fixing
Emergency prayer meetings.
For which nation?
Go, love one another...
Set your house in order...
Then, pray fireworks

Injuries in the periphery

(The place of regression, far from the centre).

Moderate or
Intermediate hunger
Blighting racism
Renewed
Again and again
Poor folks
Asking for liberty
Opportunities
So rare
Kwashiorkor
Ravaging
Indoctrinating
Incantations
Revealing darkness
Nothing to gain
We think we know

Capacity for Sensitivity

Think
Think again
Care
Love
For the poor
For the vulnerable
For the sick
For the weak

Think
Think again
Care
Love
For the homeless
For the hopeless
For the confused
For the abused

Think
Think again
It could be one
It could be the other
It could be any day
Who knows
The plans
Of uncertain storms?

Why is life like this?

You thought you planted onions
Then nettles took over
When you tried again
The weeds thought
They knew better
Crippling your thoughts
Why, why is life like this?

You thought you'd arrived
Saw all the clear signs
Departure came knocking sore;
And you thought you won,
But loss came asking
To frame and strain
Why, why is life like this?

Just when you thought
You were all united
The other party dug in
Brandishing sour songs
Soiling things sore
Pretending to be kind
Why, why is life like this?

Why should you expect one
Then see another?
Why should you do good
Then the counter calls them evil?
Triggering you to try again
Why, why is life like this?
Why?

Capacity for stress

You're itching
Your body itching
You want to do this
You want to do that
Here
There
That
This
You copycat
Rubber-neck
Climb all trees
Get stuck in everything
Make a mess of everything
Worrying
Moaning
Achieving nothing
Clustered with everything
Stop
Stop
Don't kill your self.
Take a deep breath
Relax

Somebody said, 'Children in England are among the unhappiest in the world...' - BBC NEWS

Are they worried
Worried about anything?
Are they surfeited?
Blaming technology?
Are they scared
Scared of everything?
Of running taps ?
Of toilets that flush?

They're brilliant
They're sensitive
They have doctors
They have psychologists

They're not living in huts
They're not using latrines
They have cool phones
They don't know fire ants
They don't chase snakes
They don't chase scorpions
They don't climb slippery trees

They don't walk for miles for water
They don't carry water on their heads
They don't swim in dirty ponds
They don't clean dirty school toilets

They don't cut the grass
They don't wash clothes by hand
They don't cook with firewood
They don't taste the bitter smoke

If they clean their mess
If they walk to the farm
If they eat dry garri for breakfast
If they eat dry garri for lunch
They will not be bored again
They will be happy; happy
Like children in my part of Africa.

We are all corrupt

They've been taking and taking
The colonial master
Took his own
His court clerk
Took his own
Those in uniform
Took their own
The robber took his own
The kidnapper took his own
The lecturer took his own
The market women greedy
Took their own
The religious oga
Took his share
The mechanics lying
Took their own
Then we asked for change
The politicians said, wait
We must take our own

Tiff Tiff – the thief

How we can tiff
Tiff anything
How we think
Nobody sees us

How we think
We know
But we do not know
That others know

How we stay focussed
On the stealing game
Perfecting antics
Justifying the same
With scriptures
With Books
With the constitution
Thinking we can
Continue forever
Hiding and stealing
Stealing and hiding
Haa - Tiff Tiff

Capacity to forget

Suddenly,
You have forgotten
When starvation
Held you
By the belt
You cried
In different languages
Calling me to help
Promising me everything
I voted
Lifted you up
Made you my Oga sir
Today you are
Pointing at me, empty
Playing with money
Washing millions down
Latrine pits
You've became drunk
Forgetting all
You promised
Forgetting all
You promised

Capacity to know

In the depths of
Our ancient buildings
Our ancient streets
Lie the truths
Of how to
Of how not to
Spoken
By generations past
Men, women
Known by the trees
Known by the sand
Of days gone
Not forgotten
For we know
For we know
Beyond these clouds
Beyond these scales
We know who we are
Where we come from
Our God given roots

Make you de tank God

When you see wetin pass you
You no fit talk
You bend your face to God
You tell God tank you
When you see wetin pass you
You no fit talk
You shine ya eyes
You tell God tank you
For air
For life
For water
For wisdom
For foolishness
For everything
Tell God
Say you tank am

Capacity to hate

You're loaded with
Excess boils
Uneducated biles
Molesting piles
Biting pains
Do you care?

You, only you
Carry the bugs
Carry the pain
Carry the strain
Gnawing your peace
Still unrepentant?

Goodness is cheap
Kindness is a penny
Love is sweeter
But you're wrapped
In hell's cloak
Forever, hating.

Peace beckons
Come;
Speak to me
Come
Repent; smile
Love all nations

Snap Narratives that people like in my part of Africa

You'll never be poor
Your God
Is not poor
Shout Amen

You will get
Sudden alerts
Shout Amen

Your enemies will die
Suddenly
Shout Amen

It will soon be
A million Naira
To a dollar
Shout Amen

Those chasing
You will fall
Yakata
Shout Amen

Your stiletto
Will not break
Your leg
Shout Amen
You will get
A brand
New car soon
Shout Amen

Somebody will
Give you a house
For free
Shout Amen

Everything
Na double double
Shout hallelujah
End of Service
Till next Sunday

The overzealous train inspector

It's raining questions
Strangely,
It's raining stress
I am fidgety
I left my ticket
I forgot my wallet

Are you a colon
Married
Comma, complicated
Or apostrophised?
Meaning, do I own a car?

Did you have it
With milk
With sugar
Or plain dry
Frosties, Tosties
Puffies, or nothing?

Are you
Passing, stopping,
Going
Or coming
Or something
Or anything?

Finally,
He forgot the question
The usual question
The very
Important question
May I see your ticket please?

The pain of self-Colonisation

If aliens
Or Others
Did this to us
We would shout
Complaining
Demonstrating
Protesting
Bitterly

They are
Taking over,
Completely;
Giving
Our brothers
Our sisters
Galling, polluting
Names, accursed

They are
Segregating
Discriminating
Making
Them wear
Garments
Of pain

Of shame
This sounds
Like
A broken record
Repeating
Repeating
An ear jarring
Tune titled:
Self-colonisation

What's the devil got to do with that?

You were drunk
You overslept
You went late to work
What's the devil got to do with that?

You hate the subject
You failed to study
You failed your exam
What's the devil got to do with that?

You clogged the track
You should know better
You crashed the train
What's the devil got to do with that?

You got your cake
You ate it all
Now you don't have it
What's the devil got to do with that?

You are filled with hatred
You are never positive
You never see the good in others
What's the devil got to do with that?

You made your choice
You asked for no help
You got it all fixed
What's the devil got to do with that?

Are we so different?

The same blood
Flows
In the Iroko tree
Flows
In the Elm tree
Sap meets sap
Bark kissing bark
Roots greeting roots

Since when,
When did things change?
The same water
That drips down your stem
Drips down mine
Man
Woman
Child

Full red blooded
No new descriptions
We, the world
So same same
So Iroko
So Elm
So human; us.
What's the difference?

Too many Teachers

We all
Want to teach
Pushing Theories
We teach, teach
Hugging
More Theories

Yet,
Many are sad
Many are hungry
Many are homeless
Many are sick
Many are lost

We're swimming
In words
We teach, teach
Hugging theories
Sinking
In our own sea
Of words

Decolonise & Develop

The bridge
Collapsed
They should know
The roads buckled
They should know
The buildings leaked
Why?

Their multiple
Knowledge
Was framed
By training
Not
By destiny

They should know
The density
The complexity
They,
The Engineers
should know

We're tired
Of blaming
The devil

We're tired
We're pained
Of being called
The Third world

Picture my part of Africa

In my part of Africa
In every street
There is a church
There is a mosque
There is a shrine

Hatred dances with
Greed
And foolishness
Is the DJ
Spinning broken records
And corruption
Comes in and out
Changing partners
Spraying cash
On the dance floor
People shout
Baba ke
Baba ke
Failing to criticise
Why?
Soon, they will shift
To the church
To the Mosque
To the shrine
Business as usual

The Super pill

The pill in me is speaking about the pill in you
The new scientific breakthrough
Working in us forever
Even when we are asleep or awake
They know what to do
All the time

The pill in me is speaking about the pill in you
That's all you need
To rejuvenate your body
The new normal,
Far different from what you think.
It will work for all mankind

The pill in me is speaking about the pill in you
Effecting chemical changes
That will make the world smile
Smile forever
Then they will take a break
They will take a break

The pill in me is speaking about the pill in you
Travelling systematically
Fixing the immune system
Injecting new chemical resources

Through the nerves, arteries,
Bursting all tumours

The pill in me is speaking about the pill in you
You can speak a new language
It may travel into your tongue
Then you would speak any language
Or you may even create a new language
and teach others to speak like you

The pill in me is speaking about the pill in you
It's travelling to your head now
Switching off your headache
Moving to your kidney,
It's detecting that alcohol or food overdose
Done - all sorted

The pill in me is speaking about the pill in you
Now it's taking care of your weary feet
You may never be tired when you walk for years
You may even move faster
Faster than the donkey
Faster than the bicycle

The pill in me is speaking about the pill in you
It's now travelling back to your stomach
To heal that incessant appetite for food
For weeks

For months
For years

The pill in me is speaking about the pill in you
Did you say you need a pee?
Even that may be suspended for days
Or even neutralised forever
It's moving downwards
What else do you think?

The pill in me is speaking about the pill in you
Triggering happiness in the brain
Triggering excitement in you
The real euphoria trigger
The ultimate problem solver
The friend of all mankind

The pill in me is speaking about the pill in you
Reading your mind and asking
Asking if the dead can be raised
Can we programme that?
Can we fix that plug?
Even if all things are possible?

Matters Arising

When all is said and done
After the noise dies down
Each one tell one
The truth
And nothing but the truth

That
Black Lives Matter
In the centre
Of their nation
And the centre
Of our nation

When all is said and done
After the marchers get home
Each one tell one
The truth
And nothing but the truth

That
Black Lives matter
In what we say
In what we do
Or how we feel

Feel about
Self-oppression
Self-colonisation
Self-mutilation
Self-brutalisation
Self-castigation
Self-demotion
Self-demarcation
Should I add corruption?

So, when our children roar
Roar on the streets
We'll be justified
Triple blessed
That we know
That we know
That Black Lives matter

Because,
We can't all roar
If we can't all soar
Truly,
We can't breathe
If we are not free

Black Lives Matter

This one wound
Unlike other wounds
Has lasted for too long
Others must not change it
Or tell our story for us
Black Lives Matter
That's the only page
The only page
I can see now

The Racist Test

When you are not interested
Interested in what I know
When you single me out
Punish me for no reason
Speaking to me
Like I'm nobody

When you set me up
To fail and falter
When you assess
Or supervise me unkindly
To disqualify me
Casting my application aside

When I'm more qualified
But you refuse to shortlist me
Looking closely at my name
When you smile
In front of me, you turn
Then call me silly names

You've tested negative
If these sins
Don't cling clearly
You've tested positive
If these sins
Do stick clearly

Epiphany

I am not a critic
Or someone
Who finds fault in others

Daily, I make silly mistakes
Like, forgetting to do this or that
Or say this or that
Or forgetting
To write those lines
When inspiration
Flashes an idea into my mind

In all these
There is that sudden realisation
That I may have offended you
Knowingly
Or unknowingly
Or stepped on toes
So terrible
That you think I am evil

I beg to say
I am sorry,
I am totally remorseful
For dancing in your lane

In such a way
That makes you unhappy

I am calling on you to dance
Dance with me
Hopefully, all these issues
Would be resolved
And our children, and their children
Will dance better than us
In a well-developed nation

www.ingramcontent.com/pod-product-compliance
Lightning Source LLC
Chambersburg PA
CBHW050946050726
47592CB00007B/2461

* 9 7 8 1 9 0 6 9 6 3 1 8 7 *